THIS BOOK BELONGS TO: